Rabbit

Chinese

Horoscope

2023

By
IChingHun FengShuisu

Table of Contents

Introduce

The character of people born in the year of the RABBIT

People born in the Rabbit year are gentle and caring. You are also a good friend and condescending person, in addition to having a kind, sweet, and affectionate nature. I dislike making others unhappy. Rabbits appreciate beauty, are artistic, and have refined taste. Despite being loved by friends and family, Rabbits remain pessimistic, fearful, conservative, and easily insecure. making it someone who dislikes change

People born this year are reserved, making it difficult to awaken the rabbit's mood. In any case, he dislikes arguing and prefers a quiet life. Frequently timid or skeptical That is, rabbits frequently have to weigh the pros and cons before deciding what to do.

Strength:

Rabbit people are well-mannered people who are always loved by everyone.

Weaknesses:
Likes to be alone dislikes loud noises, is easily startled, and can be overly timid at times.

Love:
People born in this year are sensitive, gentle, fanciful, and less firm in their love. If you want to love someone born in the year of the Rabbit, you must be willing to endure some pain. Don't expect the bunnies to last. He or she has a weak heart. If someone comes to do good deeds with them, they are enthralled and can't take their eyes off them. People born this year are notoriously envious. Because if you love someone, you usually won't let anyone else take it away from you. People born in this year prefer to always create an atmosphere of new love. couples born this year There is no boredom or emotionlessness. It also has a strong love mood.

Suitable Career:
People born in the Year of the Rabbit belong to the Wood element. Known occupations are thus primarily related to wood, such as tree

planting, landscaping, furniture making, wood trading, or work related to business trips related to telecommunications or work that requires extensive contact and negotiation with people, such as guides. Create a tour company, hire a DJ, and work in public relations. Department coordination, sales, creative, selling mobile phones or satellite dishes, and so on, including export business and dealing with foreigners. All of these occupations are appropriate for the Year of the Rabbit.

Year of the RABBIT (Earth) | (1939) & (1999)

"The RABBIT in the Wild" is a person born in the year of the RABBIT at the age of 84 years (1939) and 24 years (1999)

Overview

The planet orbiting your destiny house this year is "Star Thep Wisdom" for the senior destiny around the age of 84, but because this year overlaps with the year of your birth, As a result, it has been severely harmed. The most important factor is personal health care. Take care not to trip and fall while walking. Even at this age, your heart is still fighting, but your body may be resisting. Please be patient as many of the decisions made this year will be carried out. Then everything will go smoothly. Physical health necessitates a special focus on food. You should also see your doctor regularly. Psychologically, you must be able to let go of your children. Allow your grandchildren to handle any problems they encounter. Don't be too picky. Blessing your children is the best thing you can do for them and yourself. Worship God to ensure that everything goes smoothly.

This year's young destiny has an auspicious star orbiting destiny's house. As a result, this is a good year to have 100 percent physical and mental strength. Able to go to work to the fullest, both as an opportunity to build oneself and look to the future, but also because it falls in a brew year, with the evil star "Kib Sua" waiting to harass. As a result, your financial affairs will face challenges that are not as smooth as you think. You should find an opportunity to pay respect to the gods of Tai tribute at the beginning of the year to alleviate the power that overlaps the year of birth and the worst events from heavy to light. It is critical not to trust friends who are persuaded to do something against the law because they may lose money while still being held criminally responsible. This year, be cautious of accidents at work and on the road.

Career and Business

Even if you fall in the year of the collision or a year that is not favorable to you, the auspicious stars, happiness, and wisdom stars will assist you. As a result, the work flows more smoothly. Many impediments were removed. As a result, it is an excellent opportunity to develop a product that increases sales. Your dedication to self-improvement and adaptability will enable you to achieve commendable results as opportunities for expansion or additional investment. But one thing I'd like to emphasize about this year's young destiny is that it's good. Don't forget the elders who have shown you mercy; don't punish them with estrangement or simply ignore them. Especially during the months when work and trade will encounter obstacles, problems are 3rd month of China (5 Apr. - 5 May.), 5th month of China (6 Jun - 6 Jul), 8th month of China (8 Sep. - 7 Oct.) and 11th month of China (7 Dec. 22 - 5 Jan. 23). Accepting work from customers, including ordering people in the administration to cause problems, should be avoided. Contract documents must be more carefully drafted to avoid future problems. Regarding the month in which your job will have a very bright opportunity, such as the 2nd month of China (6 Mar. – 4 Apr.), the 6th month of China (7 Jul. – 7 Aug.), the 9th month of China (8 Oct. – 6 Nov.) and the 10th month of China (7 Nov. – 6 Dec.)

Financial

This year's financial situation is not stable, despite a relatively good income inflow from salary or sales of goods and services. However, what is concerning is that poor management, such as investing in risky businesses or failing to set aside funds for emergencies, can lead to major problems in managing money in the wrong pocket. Turnover is a business expense that if not saved for unforeseen expenses, can cause a liquidity problem. Particularly during months of financial deflation, namely, the 3rd month of China (5 Apr. – 5 May), the 5th month of China (6 Jun. – 6 Jul.), the 8th month of China (8 Sep. – 7 Oct.), and 11th month of China (7 Dec. 22 – 5 Jan. 23)

Fate should avoid gambling and gambling, as well as not borrowing money or guaranteeing anyone. As for the months when your financial situation will improve, such as the 2nd month of China (6 Mar. - 4 Apr.), the 6th month of China (7 Jul. - 7 Aug.), the 9th month of China (8 Oct. – 6 Nov.) and the 10th month of China (7 Nov. – 6 Dec.).

Family
The family's fortunes are not good because of the bad stars. (Lord of Destruction) is orbiting over the house of destiny, causing discord in the family. There may be a criterion for the young destiny to mourn the elder relatives. As a result, the health of the elderly at home must

be strictly monitored and given special attention. Furthermore, keep in mind that there will be disagreements among members of the house. Especially during the months when the family will encounter chaos, such as the 3rd month of China (5 Apr. – 5 May.), the 5th month of China (6 Jun. – 6 Jul.), the 8th month of China (8 Jul. - 7 Oct.) and the 11th month of China (7 Dec 22 - 5 Jan 23). You should be cautious of accidents and unforeseen events that may occur to members of the household, and you should inspect the equipment regularly. The appliances are always in good working order. In addition, keep an eye out for stolen valuables or intruders.

Love

This year, a cheerful star is orbiting to visit us. As a result, love and marriage will be new and delicious. You will be especially attractive and frequently attracted to the opposite sex. Lovers or spouses are more likely to pay close attention. Chances are good for those of you who are single and want to confess to someone you like. However, you must understand how to capitalize on your sincerity. Especially during the month in which you are promoted, including the 2nd month of china (6 Mar. – 4 Apr.), the 6th month of China (7 Jul. – 7 Aug.), the 9th month of China (8 Oct. – 6 Nov.) and the 10th month of China (7 Nov. – 6 Dec.), but if it enters the 3rd month of China (5 Apr. – 5 May), the 5th month of China (6 Jun. – 6 Jul.), 8th month of China (8 Sept. – 7 Oct.) and 11th month, China (7 Dec. 22 – 5 Jan. 23), which are the months when love can easily get into trouble and lead to disappointment It's also best to avoid getting caught up in the love of others. Furthermore, be wary of third-party intervention as a cause of disregard.

Health

This year, young people should be cautious because alcohol, cigarettes, and other drugs will cause a lot of trouble. You can also get hurt while working with or around machinery, including driving a car. You should pay more attention and care, especially in the coming months, 3rd month of China (5 Apr. - 5 May), 5th month of China (6 Jun. - 6 Jul.), 8th month of China (8 Sep. – 7 Oct.) and 11th month of China (7 Dec. 22 – 5 Jan. 23) This year, seniors must be strict about walking. Be cautious of falling and falling. Going out of the house should be accompanied by a companion. Food hygiene must be maintained. Get enough sleep and schedule annual check-ups with your doctor.

Year of the RABBIT (Gold) | (1951) & (2011)

" The RABBIT in the House" is a person born in the year of the RABBIT at the age of 72 years (1951) and 12 years (2011)

Overview

Even this year, there will be a Hokchae star for the senior destiny around the age of 72. (Dao Sukwasana) orbit to promote However, due to the presence of the dangerous planet "Keep Sua" and the chaotic power "Kak," this year has been designated as a birth year. This year, you should be aware of health and accident issues. Particularly hidden diseases that will appear this year, and should be cautious about food to avoid food poisoning. Diseases of the digestive system Stomach and intestinal issues are possible. Both should avoid sugar at all costs. Reduce your intake of fat and salty foods, as these can contribute to heart disease, high blood pressure, and kidney disease. Be wary of leg and knee problems, and the most important thing is to learn to let go and not worry about your children because it can affect your physical health.

Because the planet orbiting your destiny this year is Dao Boon Chiang (Dao Chao Panya), your academic performance will be supported by Dao overall this year. Good luck with your progress. Fate, on the other hand, should be diligently reviewing the lesson. If you don't understand something, ask the teacher to help you raise your learning level to the intended level. However, because it is the year that falls on the year of birth, there will be some complications, namely, making friends. Don't let your friends mislead you, and be wary of unforeseen accidents from activities that involve injury.

This year, both the youth and the elders, because it was the year of birth. You should make time at the start of the year to pay homage to the Tai tribute gods. (God who protects destiny) to alleviate misfortunes and turn bad things into auspicious things.

Career and Business
This year's work environment will face challenging business activities, and competition to cut prices will cause problems in a variety of ways. You should therefore look for an heir to take over the work, pass on the experience, and allow him to learn from real-world experience as you get older. Especially during the months when you must set up and work hard, such as the 3rd month of China (5 Apr. – 5 May), the 5th month of China (6 Jun. – 6 Jul.), the 8th month of China (8 Sep. – 7 Oct.) and 11th month of China (7 Dec. 22 – 5 Jan. 23). Obtaining employment in a variety of fields. Making legal acts, such as a contract document, should be carefully considered so

that you do not have to regret it later. In terms of the months in which both the work and education of the destiny are more prosperous in both life cycles, they are the 2nd month of China (6 Mar. - 4 Apr.), the 6th month of China (7 Jul. - 7 Aug.) 9th month of China (8 Oct. – 6 Nov.) and 10th month of China (7 Nov. – 6 Dec.)

Even Dao Boon Chiang's wisdom will aid in the advancement of learning for the young. But beware of the temptation to take the wrong path with easily accessible technology, so ask your parents or guardians to take good care of the child because the child's inexperience will make it easier to be right. incorrect leadership.

Financial

It does not fight well because of the fall in the year that does not support your finances. Elders should be cautious of unforeseen expenses and financial leaks. Furthermore, money and valuables should not be worn as decorations to entice thieves because they can be easily robbed and injured. Spending should be conservative to avoid a financial crisis.

Particularly during the month in which stiffness occurs, namely, the 3rd month of China (5 Apr. - 5 May), the 5th month of China (6 Jun. - 6 Jul.), the 8th month of China (8 Sep. – 7 Oct.) and the 11th month of China (7 Dec. 22 – 5 Jan. 23).

Be wary of bad debts resulting from credit issuance. You must be cautious of being duped by greed and avoid interfering with bad business. Both age cycles will have financial luck in the month in which the destiny, including the 2nd month of China (6 Mar. – 4 Apr.), the 6th month of China (7 Jul. – 7 Aug.), the 9th month of China (8 Oct. – 6 Nov.) and 10th month of China (7 Nov. – 6 Dec.).

Family

This year has not been kind to the family. It's because evil stars are aiming for the family's home. Furthermore, destiny occurred in a year that overlapped with the year of birth. As a result, things in your home should not be underestimated; be aware of health issues, and be wary of unforeseen bad events, such as accidents that may occur to members of the household. Conflicts between family members and neighbors over property or the division of inheritance among offspring. Families will face a lot of chaos in the coming months, especially during the month, the 3rd month of China (5 Apr. - 5 May), the 5th month of China (6 Jun. - 6 Jul.), the 8th month of China (8 Sep. - 7 Oct.) and 11th month of China (7 Dec. 22 - 5 Jan. '23). Keep an eye out for minors or thieving servants. This year, you should focus more on the well-being and safety of your family members. If the source of disagreements with others begins to escalate, it may be necessary to compromise to bring the event to a close.

Love

This year is ideal for taking a spouse on a trip to pay homage to the gods for the senior destiny. Furthermore, taking part in the merit-making ceremony will help to clear the mind and allow many good things to unfold. However, fate should be cautious in the coming months: 3rd month of china (5 Apr. – 5 May), 5th month of china (6 Jun. – 6 Jul.), the 8th month of china (8 Sep. - 7 Oct.), and the 11th month of China (7 Dec 22 - 5 Jan 23). Avoid getting involved in other people's families and avoid getting involved in their arguments. Listening to one side without checking the facts will raise the temperature in the house.

Health

Because there is a dangerous planet in the fated house, health is essential. As a result, the Elder Fate should be aware of any health issues. Problems with the liver, kidneys, stomach, legs, and knees are particularly common. In which the fate of both ages must take special care, especially during the following months, namely, the 3rd month of China (5 Apr. - 5 May), the 5th month of China (6 Jun. - 6 Sep.), the 8th month of China (8 Sep. - 7 Oct.) and 11th month of China (7 Dec 22 - 5 Jan 23). Accidents can happen anywhere, including at home. Crossfire is affected by unexpected disasters.

Year of the RABBIT (Water) | (1963)

" The Dharma rabbit" is a person born in the year of the RABBIT at the age of 60 years (1963)

Overview

For fate around the age of 60, because he received the power of chaos this year. Throughout the year, he had to deal with a lot of chaos. The misfortunes that existed were relieved thanks to the house of fate and the auspicious stars of wisdom (Boon Chiang) and Sukwasana (Hokchae). However, this year's work and business should not be emotionally charged. Be cautious of illnesses associated with liver disease. Heart disease and high blood pressure Furthermore, fate should exercise caution when it comes to food. Should avoid eating food with hot elements, such as barbecue grill food, and should practice good drinking and eating hygiene. Be wary of diseases that will manifest this year as a result of overindulgence. Also, be cautious of workplace accidents and avoid attending funerals.

You should make time at the start of the year to pay your respects to the gods and the Tai tribute gods. It will enable you to break through the brewing power and reveal only auspicious things and good luck. In addition, as time allows, they should seek out opportunities to practice meditation. It will aid in the reduction of health issues. And you should plan your affairs carefully to avoid problems that will cause you to be concerned later.

Career and Business

In terms of destiny's work, this year is considered prosperous because auspicious stars Boon Chiang and Dao Sam Tai are supporting and promoting it. Thinking, reading, or doing anything, so that patrons can assist. As a result, this year is ideal for expanding trade, increasing sales, increasing productivity, and looking for an heir to help carry on the work. It will become even more expandable as a result. There will be prosperity and progress on the way to work. Please remain diligent, develop, and improve to keep up with the events; this will yield positive results. However, there will be problems and obstacles during the month that you must be cautious of work, including the 3rd month of China (5 Apr. - 5 May), the 5th month of China (6 Jun - 6 Jul), the 8th month of China. (8 Sep. - 7 Oct.), and 11th month of China (7 Dec. 22 - 5 Jan. 23) Accepting a job, ordering a job, or executing contract documents, the fate should be especially cautious. So that it does not cause headaches or damage in the future. You should also avoid interfering in the affairs of others who are unrelated to you. The months in which the company made good progress were: the 2nd month of China (6 Mar. - 4 Apr.), the 6th month of China (7 Jul. - 7 Aug.), the 9th month of China (8 Oct. – 6 Nov.), and 10th month of China (7 Nov – 6 Dec).

Financial

Even though direct cash flows from salaries or sales continue to flow in, your finances remain quite sluggish this year. However, when it comes to gambling, one must be cautious of capital outflows. With and without known causes Also, be cautious not to fall into the trap of seducing money exploitation. You have the right to lose your property if you become overly greedy and get lost fraudulently. By the month that your financial fortunes are gloomy, for example, the 3rd month of China (5 Apr – 5 May), the 5th month of China (6 Jun – 6 Jul), the 8th month of China (8 Sep. - 7 Oct.) and the 11th month of China (7 Dec 22 - 5 Jan 23) prohibiting others from borrowing or receiving guarantees, as well as prohibiting investments in businesses that are biased against the country's illegality The months when your finances are in order are: 2nd month of China (6 Mar. – 4 Apr.), 6th month of China (7 Jul. – 7 Aug.), 9th month of China (8 Oct. – 6 Nov. 6) and the 10th month of China (7 Nov. – 6 Dec.).

Family

This year's family horoscope is a tight fit. You should go to pay your respects to the Tai tribute gods at the start of the year. (Annual deity of fortune protection) by performing a ceremony to cleanse the body of the harassment and depositing the date of birth at a temple or shrine where the god Tai tribute is enshrined. The stars of Hokchae can even help the house of destiny. However, evil stars are spreading their influence, so they must be wary of the little ones causing havoc. Arguments in the house ruined and harmed the peace. This year marks a significant 60th anniversary. Organizing your birthday or a wedding for a child Use the auspicious to ward off bad luck; it will aid in repairing the power of brewing in another way. Please, however, exercise caution during the following months: 3rd month of China (5 Apr. – 5 May), 5th month of China (6 Jun. – 6 Jul.), 8th month of China (8 Jul. - 7 Oct. 7), and the 11th month of China (7 Dec. 22 - 5 Jan. 23) that you should beware of lost or stolen valuables.

Love

The love story of the year is mediocre. Although there were some disagreements, it was not a major issue. They also look out for one another. However, if entering the 3rd month of China (5 Apr. – 5 May), the 5th month of China (6 Jun. – 6 Jul.), the 8th month of China (8 Sep. – 7 Oct. .), and the 11th month of China (7 Dec. 22 – 5 Jan. 23). The fate should avoid interfering with other people's families. They should also avoid going to places of entertainment that sell services. Because being infected will bring shame to your children Both will lead to family squabbles. You must also be firm. Listen to neither malicious gossip nor one side of the story.

Health

Your health has been excellent for the first six months. However, there will be problems in the last six months due to the orbiting of an unfortunate star that threatens the health base, causing disease or unforeseen dangers. You must take special care of your health, especially during the 3rd month of China (5 Apr. - 5 May), 5th month of China (6 Jun. - 6 Jul.), 8th month of China (8 Jul. - 7 Oct.), and the 11th month of China (7 Dec 22 - 5 Jan 23). Be cautious of workplace accidents. Using tools, traveling, sifting through overhead kiosks, or walking on uneven sidewalks can result in serious injury, and food poisoning should be avoided.

Year of the RABBIT (Wood) | (1975)

" The RABBIT on the moon" is a person born in the year of the RABBIT at the age of 48 years (1975)

Overview

Hokchae stars will appear in your destiny house this year. (Dao Sukwasana) orbited, but because it fell in a year of a collision or bad luck, and also discovered chaotic power, "Kak" was classified as a year of trespassing against the god Tai tribute. (The deity who protects the year's destiny), so at the start of the year, destiny should make time to pay homage to and respect the gods. Tai tribute will assist in easing the disaster that will affect you this year. This year will be difficult to avoid trouble for a business, family business, and the health of destiny. As a result, you should be mentally prepared to deal with problems and plan because many tasks will appear as obstacles as you think. In terms of finances, this year is rather fast-paced, left-handed, and right-handed, and there is a risk of a lack of liquidity in several months. Furthermore, you must exercise caution or face headaches from litigation. However, for those who work full-time or are in government service, Dao Hokchae will contribute this year. Destiny will have the opportunity to increase their salary or get a promotion, as well as move or change jobs to take on new responsibilities.

Career and Business

Jobs and trades are not stagnant this year. In addition to trying to increase twice as much, destiny will need to pay more attention to knowledge in various fields. Because of the fast-paced nature of the world, you must adjust accordingly to keep up with the currents around you. Otherwise, you will be confronted with numerous problems and obstacles, so we urge you to use your mind to solve them with caution. Every decision should not be hasty. Management must adhere to the principles of integrity and sincerity, whether dealing with subordinates, colleagues, or outsiders, both partners and customers must adhere to the principles of honesty and goodness that you uphold. It will assist you in overcoming unexpected obstacles and dangers that you will face. You should, however, exercise caution. During the months when you are not supported, namely, the 3rd month of China (5 Apr. - 5 May), the 5th month of China (6 Jun. - 6 Jul.), the 8th month of China (8 Sep. – 7 Oct.) and the 11th month of China (7 Dec 22 – 5 Jan 23) that during this time must be cautious of large events that are beyond their control. A series of events will occur that will have a direct impact on your work. Be wary of interpersonal conflicts or attempts by others to undermine organizational unity.

The months in which work and business progress and prosper are 2nd month of China (6 Mar. - 4 Apr.), 6th month of China (7 Jul. - 7 Aug.), 9th month of China (8 Oct. – 6 Nov. 6), and the 10th month of China (7 Nov. – 6 Dec.).

Financial

This year's financial situation is dire. fluctuates throughout the year, and he frequently encounters large, unexpected expenses. Now that liquidity is good, we're stuck. As a result, you should avoid gambling, gambling, and speculation in a variety of areas.

Furthermore, large-scale joint ventures with others should be carefully considered. Don't just look at the bright side because you have the right to hurt yourself. Especially during the months when your financial fortunes are bleak and you need to be extra cautious, namely, the 3rd month of China (5 Apr - 5 May), the 5th month of China (6 Jun. - 6 Jul.), the 8th month of China (8 Sep. – 7 Oct.) and 11th month of China (7 Dec. 22 – 5 Jan. 23) prohibits lending or accepting guarantees to assist others. Do not invest in businesses that are derogatory to the country's illegal activities, due to the possibility of prosecution. Neither should they invest in high-risk ventures. Because there is a greater risk of losing money than of gaining money. For the month in which your financial fortunes shine brightly, such as 2nd month of China (6 Mar. – 4 Apr.), 6th month of China (7 Jul. – 7 Aug.), 9th month of China (8 Oct. – 6 Nov.) and the 10th month of China (7 Nov. – 6 Dec.).

Family

Destiny's relatives It was relatively quiet for the first six months of this year. However, be wary of unexpected events in the second half of the year. Kip Sua works and orbits to focus on the house of destiny because it is the time of the evil star. As a result, you should be cautious of accidents that may occur among household members. Furthermore, one must be wary of malicious friends who may leave illegal items with family members or are suspected of being an accomplice to the alleged offender, causing reputational harm. The source of the domestic disorder. You need to be very careful, especially during the following months: 3rd Month of China (5 Apr.- 5 May), the 5th Month of China (6 Jun.-6 Jul.), 8th Month of China (8 Sep. – 7 Oct.), and the 11th month of China (7 Dec. 22 – 5 Jan.23). In addition, you must look after members in such situations. We still need to figure out how to keep burglars from breaking into the house and stealing things. Be cautious that family members receive unexpected incidents from close friends or lost children to lose money from others.

Love

This year, the fate of love meets a monsoon, and what both of you are stuck with, any frustrations with each other, should turn around and talk rather than using only emotions. As a trigger, there will be issues relating to sex tourism in particular. Third-party affairs and listening to incitement from others will also cause a break in the marriage. So, this year, devote more time and attention to your loved one. They must also forgive some past transgressions. Because it falls in the birth year, there are often chaotic events that cause the mind to become unstable. Especially the months when love is quite fragile, such as the 3rd month of China (5 Apr. - 5 May), the 5th month of China (6 Jun. - 6 Jul.), the 8th month of China (8 Sep. – 7 Oct.) and the 11th month of China (7 Dec. 22 – 5 Jan. 23) Avoid clashes and don't listen to one side so much that you overlook the bonds that connect them. for a long time Furthermore, you should exercise caution and avoid wandering in entertainment venues because it may not only cause problems but will spread disease.

Health

Regarding your body's health this year, the auspicious stars shining make you feel at ease and free of disease for the first six months. However, the infestation of star dumplings and the brewing year had an impact on the second half of the year. There will be unanticipated health issues and accidents. Heart disease is a disease that fate must pay special attention to. This year, foods such as grilling, barbecue, and various high-fat foods have been linked to diseases of the trachea and esophagus. You should consume fewer calories. The months in which you should prioritize your health are as follows: 3rd month of China (5 Apr. – 5 May), 5th month of China (6 Jun. – 6 Jul.), 8th month of China (8 Nov. - 7 Oct.) and the 11th month of China (7 Dec 22 - 5 Jan 23).

Year of the RABBIT (Fire) | (1987)

" The rabbit at the full moon" is a person born in the year of the RABBIT at the age of 36 years (1987)

Overview

Even this year, the planet orbiting your destiny house is a wise star. However, because the year coincides with the year of birth, it is considered a transgression against the Tai tribute gods. Furthermore, there are evil stars "Bao Chui" (explosion star) and "Xiaoying star" (star satellite) orbiting in the fated house. As a result, they frequently encounter inconsistencies in many intended matters. In making decisions for this year's work or business, you should exercise caution. It should not be done hastily because it will cause significant damage. Despite the obstacles that await, this year's work and business. But thankfully, there is an auspicious star, Thep Panya, to assist. There is still a positive result when adding and subtracting, so don't be discouraged if more determination and diligence result in progress waiting.

However, this year, the best way to help you solve the problem is to follow the principles of integrity and maintain good human relations with colleagues at both the supervisory and subordinate levels.

Career and Business

This year's destiny business is going swimmingly. Those of you who work full-time or in the government will have the opportunity to be promoted or move to a better job, and those who want to start your own business will find that this is a good time to do so. After a long period of accumulating both capital and experience. However, because this year in his destiny's house has been focused on both the lawsuit and the unlucky star "Bao Chui" (explosion star), you must be extremely cautious and prudent. Concerning the work conflict until a lawsuit is filed. Especially during the following months, which are: the 3rd month of China (5 Apr. – 5 May), the 5th month of China (6 Jun. – 6 Jul.), the 8th month of China (8th Sep. – 7 Oct.), and the 11th month of China (7 Dec. 22 – 5 Jan.23). Furthermore, when signing contract documents for procurement, employment, or any other contract this year, beware of obsessive speculations that will put you at a disadvantage, and be aware of copyrighted products. or you will be prosecuted for tax evasion. As for the month that you will have luck in work and investment: 2nd month of China (6 Mar. – 4 Apr.), 6th month of China (7 Jul. – 7 Aug.), 9th month of China (8 Oct. – 6 Nov.) and 10th month of China (7 Nov. – 6 Dec.).

Financial

This year, more financial stars are orbiting to join the fated house. Cash flow comes in two forms: directly from salaries and wages or indirectly from sales. Extra money is also available from commissions, dividends, profits from real estate or other securities, or money from good fortune. Given that the financial fortune is quite wealthy. But he couldn't ignore the evil star Bao Chui (explosion star), which would cause a large amount of money to flow out in an instant. Furthermore, if you have money and are arrogant, you will forget the benefactor who assists you. As a result, no matter how much money you have, it will not last long and may even turn negative. The period that should be especially careful about finances is the 3rd month of China (5 April – 5 May), the 5th month in China (6 Jun. – 6 Jul.), the 8th month in China (8 Jul. - 7 Oct.), and the 11th month of China (7 Dec. 22 - 5 Jan. 23) that you should spend economically. Do not allow others to borrow money and receive financial guarantees.

As for the months in which your finances flow smoothly, they are 2nd month in China (6 Mar. – 4 Apr.), 6th month in China (7 Jul. – 7 Aug.), 9th month in China (8 Oct. – 6 Nov.) and the 10th month of China (7 Nov. – 6 Dec.).

Family

Even if your family's horoscope for this year is auspicious, he was born in a lunar year. As a result, an auspicious event with a happy story conceals a job with regrets and sorrows. What you should be concerned about are the elders' health issues and any accidents that may occur among the household members. As a result, you should look for ways to avoid potentially disastrous events. Especially during the 3rd month of China (5 Apr. – 5 May), the 5th month of China (6 Jun. – 6 Jul.), the 8th month of China (8 Sept. – 7 Oct.), and the 11th month of China (7 Dec. 22 – 5 Jan. 23). In addition, beware of minors causing chaos.

Love

The love of Chao Destiny falls on Dao Tho Huai's seat this year. As a result, you can easily swerve out of the way. Be wary of allowing yourself to be led astray or speculating on gambling. As a result, there are frequent misunderstandings with your loved one's spouse. Some things are minor, but emotions can lead to major consequences. As a result, you should pay close attention. Especially during the months that do not support you, such as the 3rd month of China (5 Apr. – 5 May.), the 5th month of China (6 Jun. – 6 Jul.), the 8th month of China (8 Jul. – 7 Oct.) and 11th month of China (7 Dec. 22 – 5 Jan. 23).

Health

This year, be healthy, but watch out for gastritis and intestinal diseases, eat and drink in moderation, and don't neglect eating and living hygiene. Take precautions against infectious diseases caused by oral indulgence. Working with machinery should be avoided if you are inebriated by liquor or pickles. Going out to a party, including driving a vehicle, should be done with caution. Don't let the alcohol get the best of you. Especially during the month, remember to include: the 3rd month of China (5 Apr. – 5 May), the 5th month of China (6 Jun. – 6 Jul.), the 8th month of China (8 Sep. – 7 Oct.), and the 11th month of China (7 Dec. 22 – 5 Jan. 23) that you should be especially conscious

and should be careful of accidents during the journey, both near and far. must be careful of injury from unexpected events.

Chinese Astrology Horoscope for Each Month

Month 12 in the Tiger Year (6 Jan 23 - 3 Feb 23)

In this month of the Year of the Rabbit, your destiny is murky and unpredictable. Because expectations can shift at any time. Conflicts with close friends or family members that are likely to escalate are major concerns. Contacting or coordinating will be difficult during this time. So, if a problem arises, you should act quickly to correct your understanding. The cost of flexibility is less severe than the cost of harshness.

The trade horoscope for this month encountered a crisis. Be wary of damage caused by errors. Because you overlooked the minor details. Investing should be avoided during this time.

This salary is not good, the income is low, the expenses are excessive, and you must be cautious of unforeseen current expenses that will not be carried over to the next pay period. When you earn money, you should always keep some aside for emergencies. During this time, you will be safe, but keep an eye out for account fraud.

Misunderstandings frequently lead to arguments in the family. Be cautious of causing trouble for the family or the children. However, if you must relocate to work this month. Alternatively, plan an auspicious event to help transform the negative energy into a positive one.

On the bright side of love, those who have a partner now have a favorable opportunity for engagement and marriage.

There may be some illnesses in health. Food poisoning should be avoided, and not getting enough rest can lead to accidents. Seniors should also be cautious of limb injuries and accidents while traveling.

Support Days: 1 Jan., 5 Jan., 9 Jan., 13 Jan., 17 Jan., 21 Jan., 25 Jan., 29 Jan.
Lucky Days: 4 Jan., 16 Jan., 28 Jan.
Misfortune Days: 3 Jan., 15 Jan., 27 Jan

Bad Days: 10 Jan, 12 Jan, 22 Jan, 24 Jan.

Month 1 in the Rabbit Year (4 Feb 23 - 5 Mar 23)

Your destiny direction has been rising this month. Businesses and trades are moving in the right direction. As a result, you should take advantage of this opportunity to increase your work and generate sales for beautiful numbers, and to see the results of your efforts. This month, you should work hard and do your best without bragging in order not to irritate others. Dedicated physical and mental energy to continuously drive work to achieve goals will aid in the work's progress.

Prosperous, good, direct income continues to flow in densely for financial fortunes, but fortune money floats even if there is a pocket full of wealth. But I must warn you that if you are too greedy, your fortune will often vanish.

The family's situation is not peaceful. There will be quarrels and arguments that will not go away. You must not react emotionally because it will have far-reaching consequences. Ask you to relax by using your mind.

On the love front, singles will find the right person. Those who already have a lover or partner should secure their position. Don't listen to people who blow their noses.

Health is generally good, but you should always practice good food hygiene.

This month's investments in various projects will yield a satisfactory return.

Support Days: 2 Feb., 6 Feb., 10 Feb., 14 Feb., 18 Feb., 22 Feb., 26 Feb.
Lucky Days: 9 Feb., 21 Feb.
Misfortune Days: 8 Feb., 20 Feb.
Bad Days: 3 Feb., 5 Feb., 15 Feb., 17 Feb., 27 Feb.

Month 2 in the Rabbit Year (6 Mar 23 - 5 Apr 23)

If you have time, you should be able to perform the salvation ceremony starting this month. Fix Chong, leave the date of birth to the god Tai tribute. to ask you to take care of yourself and keep yourself safe from disaster. This month's karma is also stacked against you. During good things, bad things appeared. As a result, you should not underestimate or overlook safety in any activity. What you should do during this time is develop your year's work and financial plans, examine past mistakes as lessons, and learn how to adjust to new ones to keep up with current events.

You are considered to have usable income for this salary fortune. It's a good way to supplement a regular income. There is a chance that the money earned from gambling will be lost. However, if you are investing a large sum of money, you should exercise caution so that you do not get hurt.

The work part must face difficulties. As a result, you should work hard and be more cautious. To keep yourself safe, avoid escalating problems. You must also closely supervise your work or trade. If a problem arises, it must be resolved as soon as possible. Don't let it get out of hand. and refrain from interfering with other people's work.

Any problems in a peaceful family will be solved by relatives.

The romantic side of things is still going well. It is an opportunity to take the koi on a sightseeing trip. Always make time to be near the love plant for it to thrive.

The health is good, but if you get sick, you will be able to find a good doctor and medicine to help you fully recover.

Support Days: 2 Mar, 6 Mar., 10 Mar., 14 Mar., 18 Mar., 22 Mar., 26 Mar., 30 Mar.
Lucky Days: 5 Mar., 17 Mar., 29 Mar.
Misfortune Days: 4 Mar., 16 Mar., 28 Mar.

Bad Days: 1 Mar., 11 Mar., 13 Mar., 23 Mar., 25 Mar.

Month 3 in the Rabbit Year (6 Apr 23 - 5 May 23)

The horoscope is experiencing monsoons this month. Job duties or trades will face stiff competition. Even though the situation appears to be in crisis and there appears to be no way out, please remain calm and calm because gradually dealing with the problem will be able to turn this crisis into an opportunity. This month's problems stem from trade issues, though some of them are solvable. However, the conflict is under a lot of pressure.

This month, you should make sure that your business dealings are preceded by virtue. Well, he's good, and we truly win on both sides. This will aid in the reduction of conflicts.

Even this salary horoscope has shifted in the right direction. However, it did not go as planned for the entire month. There is a possibility of losing more in speculative gambling. You will not lose your wealth if you are not greedy for the wealth of others.

On the family front, peace, harmony, and warmth in the home will motivate you to maintain a positive attitude and move forward without feeling discouraged. But this month, when it comes to other people's families, don't waste your time getting involved. It may cause issues.

It's like water seeping into a sand pit for this love. What had been hoped for had yet to be realized. You must continue to try for some time.

In terms of health, you must be cautious of disease-causing foods, as well as accidents while traveling.

In terms of working or investing, this period has a good chance of recovering, but not significantly.

Support Days: 3 Apr., 7 Apr., 11 Apr., 15 Apr., 19 Apr., 23 Apr., 27 Apr.
Lucky Days: 10 Apr., 22 Apr.
Misfortune Days: 9 Apr., 21 Apr.
Bad Days: 4 Apr., 6 Apr., 16 Apr., 18 Apr., 28 Apr., 30 Apr.

Month 4 in the Rabbit Year (6 May 23 - 5 Jun 23)

This month, the road of his life has taken a better turn, aided by auspicious stars shining brightly. As a result, the horoscope floor is smooth and bright. Any issues will be resolved. Here are some things you should do this month: Find a way to educate yourself on what you lack and make plans for the future.

During this time, your business horoscopes found a patron. As a result, it is a good opportunity to compete in this rhythm, accelerate the project to increase work, create sales, and expand the production base and customer base because various operations will flow smoothly for both adults and subordinates during this period. Support can bring forces together in the same direction. As a result of increased total work, sales and revenues are also up.

This is an excellent time for collaboration and external investment. You can invest.

This salary fortune is favorable. You will have plenty of money to spend. However, be cautious when spending money. Don't spend until your wallet is empty before the end of the month.

Inside the family, everything is calm and happy.

The astrological sign of love. Those who are still single have the opportunity to meet the person they are interested in, and those who are already married may decide to ring the wedding bell during this time. It is regarded as a favorable time.

In terms of health, relatives and friends will be extremely helpful during this time.

Support Days: 1 May., 5 May., 9 May., 13 May., 17 May., 21 May., 25 May., and 29 May
Lucky Days: 4 May., 16 May., and 28 May.
Misfortune Days: 3 May., 15 May., 27 May.
Bad Days: 10 May., 12 May., 22 May., 24 May.

Month 5 in the Rabbit Year (6 Jun 23 - 6 Jul 23)

The fate threshold has dropped dramatically this month. There will be problems and obstacles in business and finance. Please exercise caution and avoid becoming the "scapegoat." When it comes to people, don't be so trusting that you forget to be cautious.

This salary fortune is average. However, you should exercise caution. You may be duped if you are extremely greedy. Avoid incurring long-term debt and be cautious of accounts receivable, which may suffer bad debts. Furthermore, assets are valuable and should be protected completely. Be wary of theft or loss.

You will be required to relocate at this point in your career. Be wary of aggressive remarks; unknowingly harassing others will jeopardize your job. The most important thing to remember during this period is to focus on your responsibilities before getting involved in the affairs of others. Because head lice may be discovered without your knowledge.

The family horoscope is good, even if there is good news coming in, but you should be patient for unexpected things to happen because your fate this month requires you to be cautious of the little ones who cause trouble and to closely monitor the health of the elderly in the house.

This stage of love is akin to riding a horse through the city. Things that come and go will pass quickly, whether they are love or not. As a result, be cautious because you may end up with more grass than beautiful flowers.

Health is good at the moment, but drinking and eating should be done with caution, restraint, and moderation to avoid unanticipated disasters.

Support Days: 2 Jun., 6 Jun., 10 Jun., 14 Jun., 18 Jun., 22 Jun., 26 Jun., 30 Jun.
Lucky Days: 9 Jun., 21 Jun.
Misfortune Days: 8 Jun., 20 Jun.
Bad Days: 3 Jun., 5 Jun., 15 Jun., 17 Jun., 27 Jun., 29 Jun.

Month 6 in the Rabbit Year (7 Jul 23 - 7 Aug 23)

This month, your destiny enters the alliance region and gains the power of auspicious stars shining in the house of fate. As a result, work and business operations are running smoothly. If you want to do something, you can do it, including cutting bamboo. The sky lit up again as the clouds dissipated.

On this occasion, you should always add diligence and new knowledge to yourself. Focus on pushing the work towards the goal and finding a way to unite the unity in the organization to move in the same direction to achieve bigger goals, and should hurry to clear up outstanding work and find new channels that others still know little about. Open new markets for the future and should analyze their strengths and weaknesses, as well as know how to extract benefits from what they are good at for use in the workplace. It should also be creative. Offer something novel to establish yourself as a market leader.

If the project is ready and the funds are sufficient, you can invest this month.

This salary horoscope, as well as direct income from salary and sales, is correct. However, money from fortune should be used with caution. If you're too greedy, you'll most likely have to lose money instead. As a result, it is preferable to avoid gambling.

There will be long-distance guests you have long missed and wished to meet within the peaceful family.

The love has been sweet during this period. Those who are still waiting for a response will receive one. It is nearly time for the heart to speak love.

In terms of health, you will experience some illnesses during this time because you will fail to take care of yourself. You should get enough sleep during this time. Don't overwork yourself.

Support Days: 4 Jul., 8 Jul., 12 Jul., 16 Jul., 20 Jul., 24 Jul., 28 Jul.
Lucky Days: 3 Jul., 15 Jul., 27 Jul.
Misfortune Days: 2 Jul., 14 Jul., 26 Jul.
Bad Days: 9 Jul., 11 Jul., 21 Jul., 23 Jul.

Month 7 in the Rabbit Year (8 Aug 23 - 7 Sep 23)
This month in the house of destiny was like being enveloped in clouds. What you should be wary of is being bullied or slandered in all of your work activities, so you can't react vigorously; you must be short-tempered to escape the darkness. What you should do is

look forward to the work of your responsibility to compensate for the obstacles that may arise in some cases. You must completely remove the bad and leave only the good.

Because your workplace has been in turmoil recently, you should do more to say less and maintain good relationships with both upper and lower-level colleagues so that they can rely on each other to help each other in the future. You should not gamble, speculate, or be greedy during this period of losing your seat, and you should not engage in illegal business. Accept no loans or guarantees.

These days, family matters are disrupting the peace. You must be wary of conflicts caused by unintended words that affect those close to you until they cause arguments, and you must be wary of subordinates who cause trouble. Also, be cautious of house accidents. Be especially cautious of elderly people who may slip and fall. As a result, you should find someone to watch over you.

In terms of love, this month is ruled by Dao Tho Huai, who is wary of temporary love. Even if it is only a phony love, it will cause problems.

In terms of health, be aware of infectious diseases as well as other latent diseases. They are not good in terms of relatives and friends.

Support Days: 1 Aug., 5 Aug., 9 Aug., 13 Aug., 17 Aug., 21 Aug., 25 Aug., 29 Aug.
Lucky Days: 8 Aug., 20 Aug.
Misfortune Days: 7 Aug., 19 Aug., 31 Aug.
Bad Days: 2 Aug., 4 Aug., 14 Aug., 16 Aug., 26 Aug., 28 Aug

Month 8 in the Rabbit Year (8 Sep 23 - 7 Oct 23)
This month marks a turning point in your life. As a result, many work activities are maintained and continued. Take care when turning the corner to change. Be wary of unusual issues and family feuds. The important thing to remember this month is that fate must learn patience. Make the small

things big to get excited about what your opponent wants, or you'll run out of things.

In terms of trade, the situation is still bleak. Conflicts with coworkers or in the chain of command can cause headaches. You should not, however, compete with anyone. Simply concentrate on your duties and work diligently. Even the trade direction is in a downward trend. However, if you remain determined and do not give up, you can enter an uptrend. It is preferable to use your actions as proof rather than be angry with those who have wronged you.

This salary is challenging, but you will pass. The tale of fortune and fortune will be told. But please, no avarice. Take care not to lose your fortune.

The situation was still tense within the family. Beware of the inattentive little servants who cause havoc. Be wary of fussy problems that have not yet been resolved; both the old and the new will follow. Arguments are common during this period of love. Do not listen to others' malicious gossip. And during this time, lovers will be a little aloof.

This period's health is not good. Money may cause relatives and friends to distance themselves from one another.

Support Days: 2 Sep, 6 Sep., 10 Sep, 14 Sep, 18 Sep., 22 Sep., 26 Sep., 30 Sep.
Lucky Days: 1 Sep, 13 Sep., 25 Sep.
Misfortune Days: 12 Sep, 24 Sep.
Bad Days: 7 Sep, 9 Sep, 19 Sep, 21 Sep.

Month 9 in the Rabbit Year (8 Oct 23 - 6 Nov 23)
Even if the aftermath of the monsoons is visible, the road of your life this month will be rescued. But all I ask is that destiny read it carefully. Living carefully can help to calm things down. This month, here's what you should do. Be cautious and composed. Stillness can assist in overcoming all uncertainties.

The direction of your work, including your business, will attract sponsors to assist you. As a result, the unsuccessful work can resume. This month is thus an excellent time to broaden your work, increase your productivity, generate sales, and accelerate your work system improvements. Find bugs and fix them faster. Those who work full-time should strive to show their work to their boss during this time to increase their salary.

This salary fortune, while improving, has a consistent flow of cash inflows. However, you should not underestimate the importance of establishing a control system to closely monitor financial accounts, cut unnecessary expenses, and always set aside a portion of money for savings.

Within the family, the horoscope falls on the seat of wealth, which is auspicious to visit. As a result, they are cheerful and full of smiles. However, falling into the sorrowful seat on the side of love should avoid going to entertainment places that will bring harm and harm to love at home. However, you should make more time for your family.

Your health during this time You frequently have a headache. Food poisoning and seasonal plagues should be avoided this month.

Support Days: 4 Oct., 8 Oct., 12 Oct., 16 Oct., 20 Oct., 24 Oct., 28 Oct.
Lucky Days: 7 Oct., 19 Oct., 31 Oct
Misfortune Days: 6 Oct., 18 Oct., 30 Oct.
Bad Days: 1 Oct., 3 Oct., 13 Oct., 15 Oct., 25 Oct., 27 Oct.

Month 10 in the Rabbit Year (7 Nov 23 - 6 Dec 23)

Your destiny criterion enters this month, the month that is an alliance to support the destiny with auspicious stars, thus helping to unravel the obstacles that have accumulated over the past several months, ease work and trade, and can smooth progress towards the future. The goal was as he imagined, and he received adequate support to complete many tasks quickly. There is something you should do on this occasion, and that is to complete the work according to the plan that you have devised. Don't move so quickly that you knock your legs over. Because doing so would be a waste of time and an unnecessary loss of assets.

The financial flow varies according to the horoscope of work. What you have worked hard for in the past will bear delightful fruit in every direction.

Good fortune floats are enough to play. Don't show your valuables or tempting items. Will have the opportunity to be cheated.

This month, the family horoscope predicts happiness and good fortune. You are eligible to receive good news about the wealth or success of your household members.

The love is sweet and cheerful. This is another auspicious month for some couples to get engaged or married.

If you get sick, you will be able to find a good doctor and medicine to help you heal.

This phase will be successful and yield satisfactory results for various collaborations or investments.

Support Days: 1 Nov., 5 Nov., 9 Nov., 13 Nov., 17 Nov., 21 Nov., 25 Nov., 29 Nov.
Lucky Days: 12 Nov., 24 Nov.
Misfortune Days: 11 Nov., 23 Nov.
Bad Days: 6 Nov., 8 Nov., 18 Nov., 20 Nov., 30 Nov.

Month 11 in the Rabbit Year (7 Dec 23 - 5 Jan 24)

This month, your fortunes are still up and down. This is due to the brewing power affecting the zodiac sign, as well as the many bad stars that are still harassing the group. As a result, destiny is unable to relieve the surveillance of the situation in trade. There are still obstacles in full view. You should work on it patiently. Maintaining good human relations with customers and those you have to deal with regularly will result in a good solution. During these months, you must maintain a tolerance for all forms of friction, sarcasm, and sarcasm to minimize conflict and gain the trust of adults.

Monsoons are the financial fortunes during this period. Having to pay for the property will be a non-issue. Speculative investments should be avoided at all costs and should not be gambled. This month, be wary of fraud, decorating your account numbers, and failing to turn the money in on time. As a result, you must continue to save throughout the various spending periods to avoid the crisis.

This month's family horoscope predicts that you will lose money on medical treatment for the elderly or home injury treatment.

In terms of love, there is a right to hope. Only show the courage to get to know or tell love.

This is not a good time to buy stocks or make investments.

Support Days: 3 Dec., 7 Dec., 11 Dec., 15 Dec., 19 Dec., 23 Dec., 27 Dec., 31 Dec.
Lucky Days: 6 Dec., 18 Dec., 30 Dec.
Misfortune Days: 5 Dec., 17 Dec., 29 Dec.
Bad Days: 2 Dec., 12 Dec., 14 Dec., 24 Dec., 26 Dec.

Amulet for The Year of the RABBIT

"Monk Xuan Zang saves all living things"

Those born in the Rabbit year this year should create and worship sacred objects. "Monk Xuan Zang saves all living things," so place it on your desk or cash register to ask His mercy. To stay cool and happy, help protect and prevent danger by spreading prestige. The work that you do is making good progress. It also aids in the blessing of business, smoothing of business, fulfillment, and increasing the flow of money, bringing peace and tranquility to destiny.

(Note: The direction in which sacred objects should be established can be viewed from the final text of your life cycle.)

Chapter one of the Department of Advanced Feng Shui discusses the gods who will descend to reside in the yearly mikeng (destiny house), who are the gods who can bring both good and bad to the fate of that year. When this is the case, worshiping the gods who come down to reside in the same year of your birth is thought to be beneficial and affect you the most to rely on the prestige of that deity. As your destiny declines and misfortune abates, you can help protect it. Simultaneously, you should pray for your blessings to help your business run smoothly. Bring you and your family luck and prosperity.

Those born in the Year of the Rabbit or Mia Keng Ruen have a fate in the sign of Bao. Because the horoscope coincides with the year of the zodiac this year. There are many unlucky stars to destroy as well. Throughout the year, there will be something to make you uncomfortable. But there will be someone to assist you. You will succeed if you have the opportunity to travel abroad, whether to study, work, or immigrate. It will be a year of anxiety about an uncertain future in love. Third parties may intervene and cause your love and marriage to fail.

Young Master of the Rabbit year, be especially cautious of limb injury. Both the near and far journey of the Year of the Rabbit's destiny cannot be careless with the accident, and during the year, you must be careful not to be deceived and unlucky from things you did not do. Be wary of children who cause havoc and become ill. If you believe you can solve it, you should make amulets and wear amulets. "Monk Xuanzang save all living things" to request his majesty's power to help eliminate disasters. to bring happiness, peace, and happiness to you and your family.

"Dharma Master Tang Xuan Zhang," whose birth name was "Hianchang Sae Dan," was from Henan Province in China. He was born a genius. He had studied the Dharma since he was a child. He eventually became ordained. It was well-known for its precepts, meditation, and wisdom until it received the patronage of King Tai Chong Emperor, the first king of the Tang dynasty. Lord Tang Taichung was a devout Buddhist. They also adore and respect Phra Hian Chang, so please accept their adoption as a younger brother. Phra Hian Chang is a striving monk. The mind is determined to give the Buddha life. By studying, researching, and collecting the teachings of the essence of Buddhism while traveling from China to the far-flung Indian subcontinent. He has traveled more than 50,000 miles in 19 years to spread Buddhism. and collecting the Tipitaka, which is a significant contribution to the people of the world as a result, he was given the name "Tang Xuan Zhang," which means "Tripitaka." He was addressed in Chinese. Worshiping the Buddha will play a part in eliminating misfortune all misfortune without a bully and finding a convenient way to conduct business and various tasks to make everything as smooth as desired and to have everything in abundance. Those born in the year of the Rabbit should also wear an auspicious pendant. "Monk Tang Xuan Zhang pleases animals" around your neck or carry it with you when traveling both locally and long distances. To fill your destiny with auspicious wealth, prosperity, and progress in business, business, business, family peace, and happiness throughout the year, resulting in better efficiency and effectiveness faster than ever.

Good Direction: Northwest, Southeast, and East

Bad Direction: West

Lucky Colors: Green, Light Blue, Black, Gray, and Blue.

Lucky Times: 05.00 – 06.59, 13.00 – 14.59, 19.00 – 21.59.

Bad Times: 07.00 – 08.59, 11.00 – 11.59, 17.00 – 18.59.

Good Luck For 2023